ELLIS SCHOOL LIBRARY

CHINA

...in Pictures

Prepared by
Stephen C. Feinstein

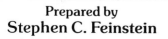

Lerner Publications Company
Minneapolis

Courtesy of Nik Wheeler/*Aramco World*

With the tail of his kite flying far behind him, a Chinese man enjoys the atmosphere in Tian'anmen Square.

This book is an all-new edition in the Visual Geography Series. Previous editions were published by
Sterling Publishing Company, New York City. The
text, set in 10/12 Century Textbook, is fully revised
and updated, and new photographs, maps, charts, and
captions have been added.

LIBRARY OF CONGRESS CATALOGING-IN-PUBLICATION DATA

Feinstein, Steve.
  China in pictures / prepared by Steve Feinstein.
    p. cm. — (Visual geography series)
  Rev. ed. of: China in pictures / Joanna Moore.
  Includes index.
  Summary: Describes the topography, history, society,
economy, and government of China.
  ISBN 0-08225-1859-7 (lib. bdg.)
  1. China. [1. China.] I. Moore, Joanna. China in pic-
tures. II. Title. III. Series: Visual geography series
(Minneapolis, Minn.)
DS706.F34 1989   88-30276
951—dc19   CIP
                                                   AC

International Standard Book Number: 0-8225-1859-7
Library of Congress Catalog Card Number: 88-30276

VISUAL GEOGRAPHY SERIES®

Publisher
Harry Jonas Lerner
Associate Publisher
Nancy M. Campbell
Senior Editor
Mary M. Rodgers
Editor
Gretchen Bratvold
Assistant Editors
Dan Filbin
Kathleen S. Heidel
Photo Researcher
Karen A. Sirvaitis
Editorial/Photo Assistant
Marybeth Campbell
Consultants/Contributors
Stephen C. Feinstein
John Philip Ness
Sandra K. Davis
Designer
Jim Simondet
Cartographer
Carol F. Barrett
Indexer
Sylvia Timian
Production Manager
Gary J. Hansen

Independent Picture Service

A Chinese craftswoman makes bamboo fans at a factory in Guizhou province.

Acknowledgments

Title page photo by Ruthi Soudack.

Elevation contours adapted from *The Times Atlas of
the World*, seventh comprehensive edition (New York:
Times Books, 1985).

Chinese proper names, which are written with Chinese
characters, have been Romanized (transcribed in the
Latin alphabet) according to the *pinyin* system. See
page six for a listing of familiar names and their pinyin equivalents.

2   3   4   5   6   7   8   9   10 98 97 96 95 94 93 92 91 90

At an outdoor stadium in Beijing (Peking) – the capital of China – participants in a sports event form gigantic designs and murals.

Contents

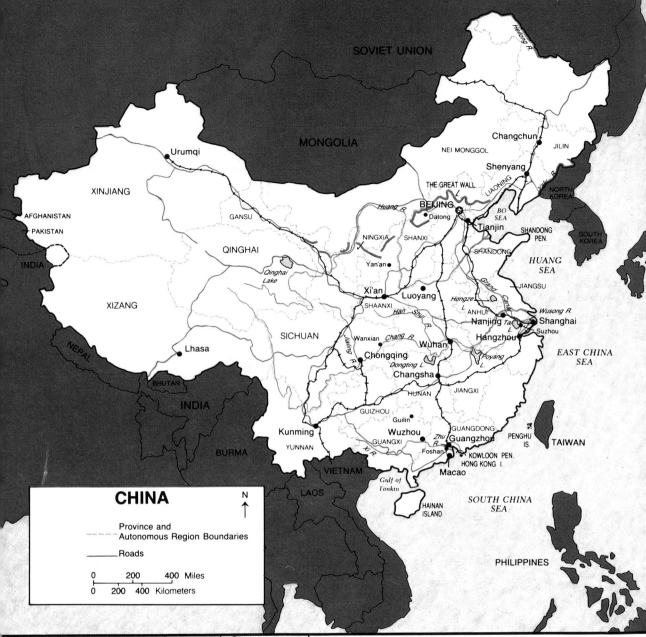

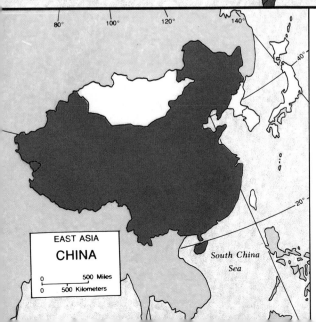

METRIC CONVERSION CHART
To Find Approximate Equivalents

WHEN YOU KNOW:	MULTIPLY BY:	TO FIND:
AREA		
acres	0.41	hectares
square miles	2.59	square kilometers
CAPACITY		
gallons	3.79	liters
LENGTH		
feet	30.48	centimeters
yards	0.91	meters
miles	1.61	kilometers
MASS (weight)		
pounds	0.45	kilograms
tons	0.91	metric tons
VOLUME		
cubic yards	0.77	cubic meters
TEMPERATURE		
degrees Fahrenheit	0.56 (*after* subtracting 32)	degrees Celsius

In Xi'an, a historic city in the province of Shaanxi, a man with his daughter carries a fish home from a local market.

Introduction

With its long history and varied landscape, China stands out among the world's countries as the most populated nation on earth. About one billion people share China's fertile plains, elevated plateaus, and arid deserts on the Asian continent. Most Chinese are farmers and herders, who struggle to feed the nation's huge population.

For over 3,000 years, powerful emperors and their court bureaucracies ran the vast Chinese Empire. Over the centuries, Chinese scientists and scholars contributed to human knowledge by inventing paper, gunpowder, and the magnetic compass and by writing classic Chinese poems and novels.

In the early twentieth century, grassroots rebellions overthrew the empire and replaced it with a republic (a regime that has no monarch). A civil war in the 1940s ended a long period of turmoil and ushered in China's Communist government. The new system raised the hopes of many Chinese for economic, political, and social reform.

Efforts in the 1950s and 1960s to modernize China and to rid its culture of foreign ideas brought hardship to much of China's population. During the Great Leap Forward of the late 1950s, expectations were high for local economic development. But, after a massive reorganization of the agricultural sector, as many as 20 million people died of starvation because of low farming productivity. The process of rejecting traditional and foreign ideas reached its peak during the Great Proletarian Cultural Revolution between 1965 and 1975.

Since the late 1970s, China has attempted to restore its economic vitality. New policies mix socialist principles —which emphasize common goals and shared landownership—with personal incentives and Western technologies. In another change of position, the Chinese government now welcomes the investments of foreign countries. Although questioned by conservative Chinese Communists, these policies may bring China the prosperity that it has long sought.

CONVERSION CHART

COMMON TERM ➡ **PINYIN EQUIVALENT**

GEOGRAPHICAL NAMES:

Common Term	Pinyin Equivalent
Canton	Guangzhou
Chungking	Chongqing
Gobi Desert	Gebi Desert
Inner Mongolia	Nei Monggol
North China Plain	Huabei Plain
Peking	Beijing
Pescadores	Penghu Islands
Szechwan	Sichuan
Tibet	Xizang
Tibet, Plateau of	Qing Zang, Plateau of
Yangtze River	Chang River
Yellow River	Huang River

HISTORICAL NAMES:

Common Term	Pinyin Equivalent
Chiang Kai-shek	Jiang Jieshi
Ch'in dynasty	Qin dynasty
Ch'ing dynasty	Qing dynasty
Chou dynasty	Zhou dynasty
Chou Enlai	Zhou Enlai
Hsia dynasty	Xia dynasty
Kuomintang	Guomindang
Mao Tse-tung	Mao Zedong
Sung dynasty	Song dynasty
Sun Yat-sen	Sun Zhongshan

GENERIC NAMES:

Common Term	Pinyin Equivalent
basin	pendi
desert	shamo
lake	hu
mountains	shan
plain	pingyuan
plateau	gaoyuan
range	ling
river	jiang, he
sea	hai

The adoption of *pinyin*—a relatively new system for converting Chinese characters into the Latin alphabet—has changed the written form of many Chinese proper names. This two-column list contains some of the most familiar common terms and their pinyin equivalents. Although there are pinyin names for generic terms, such as river and mountain, only proper names appear in pinyin in this book. For clarity, generic names are in English.

Courtesy of Carl Wilcox

In mountainous northwestern China, a camel driver guides his animals through largely uninhabited land.

1) The Land

China, officially called the People's Republic of China (PRC), is one of the largest countries in the world. Only the Soviet Union and Canada exceed China in size. With about 3.7 million square miles of territory, China is almost as big as the entire continent of Europe. Its one billion people make up one-fifth of the earth's human inhabitants.

The Soviet Union, the largest of China's 11 neighbors, borders China to the northwest and the northeast. Mongolia intrudes between China and the Soviet Union in the north. To the west are Afghanistan, Pakistan, and India. Natural barriers, such as mountains and thick forests, separate China from Nepal, Bhutan, Burma, Laos, and Vietnam in the south. Along China's northeastern border with North Korea, overland travel is fairly easy. The nation's southeastern and eastern boundaries lie along the South China, East China, and Huang (Yellow) seas, which are linked to the Pacific Ocean.

According to agreements reached in 1984, Britain will return the island of Hong Kong to Chinese control in 1997. The small colonial outpost has been under British authority since 1842.

The Turpan Depression lies in the northeastern Tarim Basin. At its lowest point, the depression is 426 feet below sea level.

China's coastline stretches for more than 7,000 miles, and many islands lie offshore, including two small outposts of European power—the British colony of Hong Kong and the Portuguese colony of Macao. Hong Kong is scheduled to return to Chinese control in 1997, and by the late 1980s negotiations for the restoration of Macao to Chinese authority had begun.

Also off China's coast is the large island of Taiwan, which, since 1950, has been the home of the Nationalist Chinese government. This group ruled China between 1927 and 1949 and continues to regard itself as the rightful government of China.

China has disputed some of its boundaries, particularly with its neighbors the Soviet Union and India. As a result, more than 10,000 miles of frontier are not settled. In addition, China—as well as other nations in the region, including Vietnam, Malaysia, and the Philippines—claims many islands in the South China Sea.

Topography

China has one of the world's most diverse landscapes. Within the nation's boundaries lie barren deserts, snowcapped mountains, and fertile coastal areas. Also of interest is the Plateau of Qing Zang (Plateau of Tibet). With an elevation of over 16,000 feet, this tableland is the highest in the world.

DESERTS

Much of western China is desert. The Autonomous Region of Nei Monggol (a partially self-governing administrative unit also called Inner Mongolia) borders the Gebi (Gobi) Desert in the north and includes the Mu Us Desert in the southwest. In an effort to help local herders, government programs have begun to protect the region's limited supply of grasslands. Workers dig wells and install electric water pumps to improve grazing conditions.

Northwestern China, including the Tarim Basin and the vast Taklimakan Desert, is also dry. Deep wells and irrigation canals water the soil. About 25,000 square miles of wasteland were made fertile in the 1970s, when the government established mechanized farms through irrigation.

MOUNTAINS

In western China, the main ranges are the Tian Mountains, the Pamirs, and the Himalayas. The peaks in these ranges are among the highest in the world. China shares the Tian Mountains with the Soviet Union. On the border between the two nations lies the range's highest point— Pobeda Peak—which is 24,406 feet above sea level. The Pamirs, a western chain with many peaks that are over 20,000 feet high, stretch into several neighboring countries.

The Himalaya Mountains—the tallest range in the world—extend for 1,500 miles between Pakistan and northeastern India. China's southern frontier includes a large

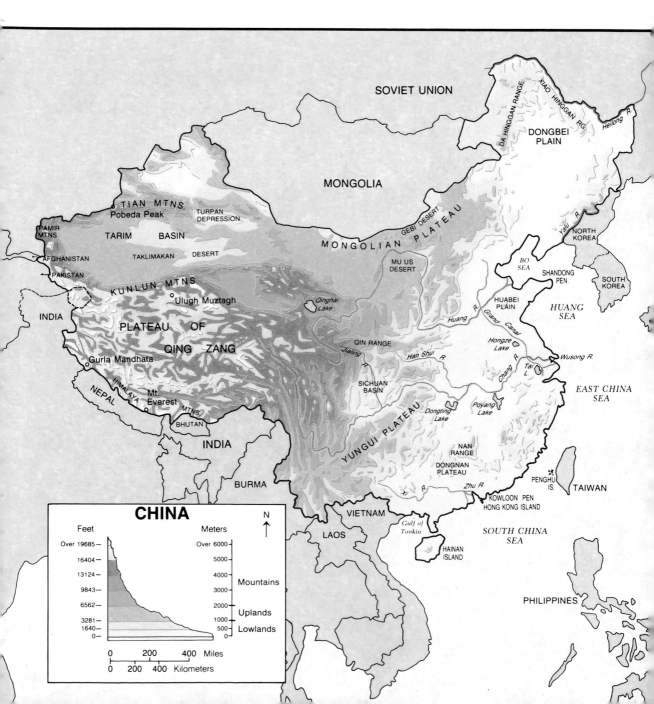

CHINA

Feet	Meters
Over 19685	Over 6000
16404	5000
13124	4000
9843	3000
6562	2000
3281	1000
1640	500
0	0

N ↑

Mountains
Uplands
Lowlands

0   200   400 Miles
0   200   400 Kilometers

Courtesy of Carl Wilcox

Trekkers ski down a slope in the Pamir Mountains toward their camp near the base of the range.

Courtesy of Mark Anderson

Near heavily etched rock formations, a boat glides along the Chang (Yangtze) River as it flows through eastern China.

portion of the Himalayas. Mount Everest (29,028 feet)—the earth's highest point—lies along the border with the Kingdom of Nepal. The tallest Himalayan mountain completely within China is Gurla Mandhata (25,355 feet).

The Kunlun Mountains run from west to east in the center of China along the northern border of Xizang (Tibet). Many ranges fan out from this chain, whose highest peak is Ulugh Muztagh, at 25,348 feet above sea level. In the northeastern corner of China lie two mountain chains—the Da Hinggan and Xiao Hinggan ranges.

EASTERN COAST

All of China's major rivers flow eastward toward the Pacific Ocean. As a result, the nation's fertile coastal regions are well watered. Not surprisingly, most of the country's population live in the east.

The Dongbei Plain and the Dongnan Plateau lie, respectively, at the northern and southern ends of the coast. Between these two points is the Huabei (North China) Plain, which is one of China's most productive wheat-growing regions. Southeastern China is known for its rice fields as well as for its tall limestone formations.

PLATEAU OF QING ZANG

The Plateau of Qing Zang lies at an average altitude of 16,000 feet. The Kunlun Mountains border the plateau on the north, and the Pamirs lie to the west. Bounded on the south by the Himalayas, the plateau includes most of the Autonomous Region of Xizang. Two of the nation's main rivers—the Huang (Yellow) and the Chang (Yangtze)—begin in the highlands of the plateau. Much of the Plateau of Qing Zang consists of barren terrain, where the region's traditional occupations of farming and herding are difficult to practice.

Rivers and Lakes

China's northernmost waterway is the Heilong River. Over its length of more than 2,000 miles, this river separates eastern China from the Soviet Union. During the 1960s, a border dispute flared between the two nations for control of the waterway. As a result, parts of the boundary in the northeast are still unsettled.

The 2,900-mile-long Huang River rises in the mountains of the north central province of Qinghai. The waterway flows parallel to the mountains and then makes a wide sweep northeast into Nei Monggol. The river eventually turns south and finally travels eastward into the Bo and Huang seas. The course of the Huang River affects the fertility of 35 million acres of farmland.

The Huang River carries vast quantities of a fine, yellow soil—called loess—that have been washed into the river from its banks. As a result, the riverbed of the Huang has risen higher over the centuries, and less water can be held within its banks. When the water overflows, devastating floods occur. For this reason, the Huang River is called "China's Sorrow."

China's longest waterway is the 3,434-mile-long Chang River, which feeds a vast

Grazing horses kick up dust on the Plateau of Qing Zang (Plateau of Tibet), where sparse grasses provide food for livestock.

11

Photo by Richard Kagen

network of irrigation ditches, providing water for northern wheat fields and southern rice acreages. The Chang River, like the Huang, originates in the province of Qinghai. The waterway flows in a torrent for hundreds of miles through canyons that it has cut into the mountains. Eventually, the river empties into the East China Sea, north of Shanghai—one of China's most important ports.

The Xi River of Guangdong province flows for 1,200 miles in southeastern China and is largely a commercial sea-lane. Large boats can navigate the Xi as far as Wuzhou, and small vessels can travel beyond this point. The Zhu (Pearl) River forms part of the Xi delta and passes through the city of Guangzhou (Canton).

River-fed lakes dot China's landscape. Among the largest is Dongting Lake, a shallow body of water in northeastern Hunan province. When the lake is full of water, it exceeds 3,500 square miles in area. Poyang Lake in northern Jiangxi province is 90 miles long and 20 miles wide. It receives the waters of many of the rivers that travel to southeastern China. Other important bodies of water include Tai and Hongze lakes in eastern China and Qinghai Lake, which lies in central China.

This section of the Great Wall of China—whose total length stretches for about 3,750 miles—follows the contours of the surrounding countryside north of Beijing.

The Great Wall and the Grand Canal

Although not a natural barrier, the Great Wall of China has stood against invaders from the north for more than 2,500 years. Begun in about the fifth century B.C. and enlarged in later periods, this high, stone wall once extended for over 6,000 miles from the Yalu River in the northeast to Gansu province in the northwest. Vandalism and erosion have reduced its length to 3,750 miles. The most visited section is near Beijing, the capital of China, and the government is restoring parts of the wall in other regions.

Although begun over 2,500 years ago, the Great Wall was substantially restored and expanded under the Ming family of rulers (1368–1644). As a military line of defense, the barrier had thousands of openings from which troops could fire weapons. The width of the wall's course could accommodate 5 horse riders or 10 foot soldiers walking shoulder to shoulder.

13

The Grand Canal connects the Huang and Chang rivers with a 1,000-mile-long route. In Beijing, the waterway remains a basic means of bringing food and other goods to the capital from the south.

Many of the boats that ply the Grand Canal are manually propelled. Some boat owners push poles against the bottom of the waterway to move their vessels. Others pull their crafts from shore.

Over 1,000 years ago the Chinese emperor Sui Wendi saw the value of controlling the flow of water in the Chang and Huang rivers. He built the world's largest artificial waterway—called the Grand Canal—between the two rivers. It continues to be a transportation route in the twentieth century. The canal stretches between Beijing and Hangzhou—a distance of more than 1,000 miles.

Climate

Many regional climatic variations exist in China, chiefly because of the nation's huge size and varying altitudes. The Plateau of Qing Zang and parts of northern China experience great extremes in temperature. In winter (November to February), temperatures may reach lows of −13° F. In summer (May to September), temperatures in these areas range between 60° and 80° F.

The provinces of central China have a milder climate, with average temperatures of 80° F in summer and 30° F in winter. The eastern parts of the great basins of the Huang and Chang rivers experience wet, hot summers (average temperature 75° to 93° F) and dry, cool winters (25° to 50° F). The deserts see highs of 100° F in summer and lows of 15° F in winter.

Eighty percent of China's total rainfall comes between the months of May and October. Monsoons (seasonal winds) bring 20 to 40 inches of annual rain to northeastern China, and southeastern regions get 80 to 120 inches per year. The deserts and the Plateau of Qing Zang receive the smallest amounts of precipitation—usually between 4 and 10 inches annually.

Because the summer rainy season in northwestern China is short, this region is dry nearly all the time. In some southern provinces, rain falls throughout the year, occasionally in amounts that can cause flooding near river basins. Coastal provinces also experience typhoons—violent hurricanes—that can destroy urban centers as well as farmland.

Because it lies between the harsh, cold areas of the north and the wet, warm regions of the south, Qinghai province has a moderate climate. Here, a small town in the province is dusted with snow in the month of February.

The Gebi (Gobi) Desert in northern China receives almost no rainfall and experiences high temperatures in the summer months.

15

Vegetation clings to the granite mountains of Anhui province. Poets and painters have long used the area's spectacular scenery—including cloud-covered peaks and twisted pine trees—as inspiration for their work.

Courtesy of Woodrow Parks

Flora and Fauna

Hundreds of years of intense farming and urban expansion have destroyed much of China's original vegetation. Only in remote mountain areas do natural forests—including stands of oaks, maples, larches, and birches—survive. Rain-forests exist south of the Chang River and contain a mixture of evergreens and palms.

Southern China features a variety of subtropical species, including bamboo trees, ginkgos (trees with fan-shaped leaves and yellow fruit), laurels, and magnolias. Western China hosts drought-resistant grasses, herbs, and desert scrub. Vegetation is somewhat more plentiful in the southwest and includes alpine grasses and mountain flowers.

The forests bordering Xizang and Sichuan are the home of the bamboo-eating giant panda. Until 1938—when some were taken to Great Britain—pandas had never been seen outside China. In Xizang, the goat, yak (a relative of the ox), and dzo are native animals. The dzo, a cross between a yak and a zebu (a humped Asian cow), also shares its habitat with the takin (goat antelope) and the musk deer.

16

Bactrian (two-humped) camels live in Xinjiang, and water buffalo are valued in southern China as work animals. The tropical regions of the nation host macaques (short-tailed monkeys) and gibbons (tailless apes). Only a few tigers and bears still roam the country, and snow leopards survive in Xizang. Hooved animals—such as gazelles, deer, and antelope—thrive in herds in the western uplands.

Alligators inhabit the rivers of east central China, and four-foot-long salamanders slither in and out of the waterways of western China. The nation's native bird population is diverse and includes peacocks, herons, and cranes.

A farmer near Foshan in Guangdong province allows her hardworking water buffalo—which are among China's primary labor animals—to cool themselves in a local stream.

Courtesy of Steve Feinstein

Courtesy of Steve Feinstein

Protected by law in China, giant pandas can weigh as much as 300 pounds. In the 1970s—when bamboo shoots, a major part of the panda's diet, were in short supply—at least one-fourth of China's panda population starved to death.

Natural Resources

China has a large variety of mineral resources. Its deposits of antimony (used in alloys) and tungsten (a hard, heat-resistant mineral) are the world's largest. The nation's reserves of lead, tin, manganese, copper, mercury, molybdenum (used to strengthen steel), and aluminum are also abundant.

Extensive amounts of coal exist in the central provinces of Shaanxi, Guizhou, and Sichuan, as well as in the northern part of Xinjiang and in the eastern province of Shandong. Abundant coal reserves have led the Chinese government to continue building steam locomotives for the railways rather than to switch to diesel engines.

Petroleum discoveries have been increasing, especially off the eastern coast. The main oil fields of western China are in Xinjiang, near the city of Urumqi. More recent sites have opened in northeastern China, and offshore drilling platforms are located in the South China Sea, the Gulf of Tonkin, and the Bo Sea.

Courtesy of Mark Anderson

Coal – China's most abundant natural resource – is loaded aboard barges on the Chang River.

Major Cities

China has many cities with more than one million inhabitants. Over one-fifth of the nation's people live in urban areas. China's three largest cities—Shanghai, Beijing, and Tianjin—are not part of any province. Instead, they are each a separate administrative unit that reports directly to the central government.

Crowded Shanghai, with approximately 12 million people, is among the five most populous cities in the world. The Wusong River divides Shanghai into two parts. The shabbier north bears signs of the Japanese occupation during World War II, while the south features many buildings reminiscent of Western cities in the 1930s. Shanghai—China's primary commercial center—is also one of the nation's most important port cities and handles much of the country's domestic and foreign trade.

Beijing (population 9.3 million)—the capital of China—lies in the northeastern part of the country. The city contains some of the nation's most important monuments and historical treasures, such as the Forbidden City, which once was the site of an imperial palace. Expansion and industrialization have changed Beijing in recent decades, and thousands of buses and several freeways now transport people and goods throughout the capital.

Beijing's colorful markets—more common since the government lifted trade restrictions in the mid-1980s—offer fruits, vegetables, meats, and consumer goods from the farms and factories of surrounding regions. Colleges and universities—including prestigious Beijing University—are scattered throughout the capital and were the hotbeds of the student unrest that erupted in 1989.

Courtesy of Woodrow Parks

A busy street in Shanghai reflects the city's commercial success as well as its crowded space.

Southeast of Beijing lies Tianjin (population 7.9 million), whose name means "entrance to the heavenly capital." Located near the Bo Sea, the city is a major transportation hub and industrial center. Along with several other coastal sites, Tianjin has been rapidly improving its port and manufacturing facilities. Large ships can now berth in the city's harbor, and local factories produce automobiles, elevators, sewing machines, and cameras.

Secondary Urban Centers

Chongqing (Chungking)—China's fourth largest city, with a population of 6.5 million—lies in Sichuan province. The name Chongqing means "repeated good luck,"

Courtesy of Carl Wilcox

Beijing contains some of China's most historic royal buildings. The Forbidden City—so-called because ordinary people were not permitted to pass through its grounds—includes the Imperial Palace. Built in the fifteenth century, the complex is now a public park.

and the city's continued growth and development may have to do with its location at the junction of the Jialing and Chang rivers. Workers on recent expansion projects have renovated Chongqing's streets, have constructed parks, and have improved urban transportation. The city's broad manufacturing base includes the making of tools, machinery, chemicals, and textiles.

Guangzhou (population 5.3 million) is the capital of Guangdong province and the most important center for international trade in southern China. Set in China's tropical region, Guangzhou is often muggy and smoggy. Its former slums and houseboats have been replaced in recent decades with new housing and better services. In addition to products from surrounding farms, the city offers factory-made items —such as cement, steel, chemicals, and fertilizers—for sale in its markets and stores. Zhongshan University, noted for its med-

ical school, is among many colleges and other institutions located in Guangzhou.

Shenyang is one of northeastern China's largest industrial cities, and the government has placed a high priority on modernizing its facilities. As a result of the area's new factories, the population increased from 100,000 in 1910 to nearly five million in 1988. Much of Shenyang has been built in the last few decades and displays a modern urban plan that includes open parks, wide streets, and skyscrapers.

Strategically located at the junction of the Han and Chang rivers, Wuhan (population 4.5 million) has developed into a major transportation and industrial hub in Hubei province. The word *Wuhan* is actually a combination of three city names—*Wu* stands for Wuchang, and *han* represents both Hankou and Hanyang. Since 1957, a bridge that spans the Chang River in central China has connected these three urban centers.

Courtesy of Woodrow Parks

A bridge connects the urban sectors of Wuhan in east central China.

Courtesy of Steve Feinstein

Bicycles and laundry clog a narrow street in Guangzhou.

A bronze ceremonial vessel dates from the late Shang period (about 1100 B.C.). The shape and carved details of the piece indicate its use in rites for the dead.

2) History and Government

Although China has one of the oldest written histories in the world, the earliest records of Chinese settlement are archaeological. Human bones, from roughly 250,000 to 500,000 years ago, were found in northern China. Archaeologists named the prehistoric species "Beijing man" and believe that he communicated by language, that he fashioned stone tools, and that he made use of fire. From these early ancestors developed Stone Age peoples—first the Yang Shao, and then the Longshan.

Centered in the valley of the Huang River, the Yang Shao culture flourished in about 3000 B.C. A more settled people—the Longshan—displaced the Yang Shao and lived by rice farming and livestock raising.

According to tradition, the Xia dynasty (family of rulers) followed the Longshan culture. Although no archaeological evidence supports its existence, the Xia period persists in Chinese legend.

Early Recorded History

The first Chinese administration for which written records exist is the Shang dynasty. Governing a largely agricultural society, the Shang dynasty controlled north central China between the eighteenth and eleventh centuries B.C. On bronze ceremonial cups and on turtle shells, members of the Shang described some of the dynasty's events in China's first written language.

The Zhou people from western China attacked and defeated the Shang dynasty in the eleventh century B.C. The Zhou dynasty lasted for almost 900 years and divided China into small, hereditary realms. These kingdoms were the property of individual warlords (local military leaders), whose close relationship to the dynasty's ruler ensured stability. The subdivision of power, however, also led to internal warfare among the many small realms.

Zhou rule continued until 221 B.C., when Qin Shihuangdi—head of a strong and extremely well-organized realm—defeated the warlords and established his capital near Xi'an. Qin Shihuangdi is regarded as China's first emperor. Inside his burial site, archaeologists found more than 8,000 life-sized terra-cotta statues that sculptors had produced as ceremonial guards for the emperor's tomb.

Under the Qin dynasty—which lasted less than 20 years—farming, livestock raising, and silk making were common livelihoods. The realm built dams and canals and had an advanced trading economy that included standardized weights and measures. Scholars, who were skilled in poetry, philosophy, music, and painting, recorded historical events.

The empire stretched from the foothills of the Mongolian Plateau in the north to the basin of the Chang River in the south. Armies of the Qin emperors advanced farther south into the coastal areas near

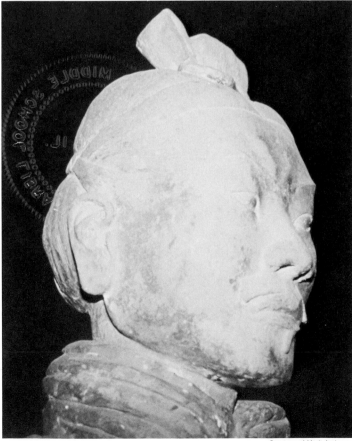

The head of a life-sized clay statue in Qin Shihuangdi's tomb shows the natural facial traits that are characteristic of the site's sculptures. Qin Shihuangdi, China's first emperor, ordered the building of his tomb in 247 B.C., when he was 13. The emperor was buried with over 8,000 individually sculpted figures, as well as with many members of his court. Well diggers discovered the tomb in 1974.

22

Buddhism arrived in China from India in the fourth and fifth centuries A.D. Near Datong in Shanxi province, a 55-foot-tall statue of Gautama Buddha—the founder of the Buddhist religion—was carved out of stone between 460 and 494.

Guangzhou and conquered what is now northern Vietnam.

Thick, high walls—which the Zhou dynasty had built earlier to keep out the nomadic peoples of Mongolia—were connected and extended to form the Great Wall. Eventually, this barrier stretched for thousands of miles from the eastern coast to far west of Gansu province. The Qin dynasty established imperial unity, which enabled the successive Han dynasty to rule without interruption for four centuries.

Han Dynasty

During the Han dynasty (202 B.C. to A.D. 220), China made further economic and cultural advances. Han rulers introduced the manufacture of paper to Korea, Japan, India, and Arabia. Scientists invented the seismograph to record movements of the earth's crust—earthquakes, for example—and made great advances in astronomy. Chinese craftspeople produced fine-quality porcelain, silk brocades, and strong wool. Envoys sent to the borderlands of the west met traders from India and Persia (modern Iran) and established the Silk Road. Similarly, the Spice Route brought China into commercial contact with Southeast Asia.

Also of importance during the Han dynasty was Confucianism, which is based on the ideas of Confucius, a philosopher of the sixth century B.C. Confucius taught that the role of rulers is to bring happiness to their subjects and that the family is the basis of all human relationships. From these ideas developed a state system run by people who were considered models of morality and who were promoted within the bureaucracy on the basis of merit.

Despite its decades of achievement, the last century of Han rule was unstable, as corruption, rivalry, and rebellion plagued the state. The Han dynasty ended in disorder in A.D. 220. Eventually, three kingdoms—the Wei, the Shu, and the Wu—emerged. But these realms shared power for only a few decades. The rival kingdoms

23

gave way to a period of splintered rule in the fourth and fifth centuries. During this time, the Buddhist religion, which had its beginnings in India, took root in China.

After more than 300 years of disunity, the Sui dynasty reunited China in the sixth century A.D. During the reign of the Sui family, the emperor Sui Wendi constructed the Grand Canal—one of the world's outstanding engineering achievements. Grass-roots rebellions and natural disasters weakened the Sui dynasty, and a rival group—the Tang—took power.

Tang and Song Dynasties

Between the seventh and ninth centuries, the Tang dynasty sponsored many economic and cultural advances, including block printing. Rulers of the dynasty began to select members of the civil service by examination. Governments from present-day Korea and Xizang recognized Chinese authority. Trade by caravans along the Silk Road extended to Samarkand (in the present-day Soviet Union) and Constantinople (now in Turkey) and went by sea to regions near the Persian Gulf.

The peak years of achievement were followed by a gradual decline in the ninth century. Heavy taxation, forced labor, obligatory military service, palace extravagance, and bureaucratic corruption once more weakened the empire. As a result of these problems, other groups were able to seize power.

For over a century, conflict and division disrupted China. But in 960 Song Taizu took power and established the Song dynasty, which reunited the empire under a strong central government. During the 300 years of Song rule, expansion of trade, urban growth, and technical progress continued. Improvements in navigational techniques brought greater maritime (seafaring) trade, and Korean, Persian, and Arab commercial communities developed in the ports of Guangzhou and Hangzhou.

Photo by Asian Art Museum of San Francisco, The Avery Brundage Collection

A diamond-shaped brick of gray pottery depicts a dancer from the period of the Tang rulers (about A.D. 650).

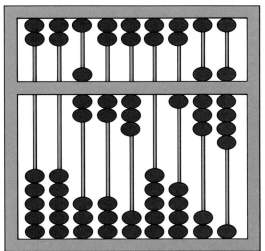

Artwork by Laura Westlund

Abaci—apparatuses that can solve arithmetic problems—first appeared during the rule of the Song emperors. Each bead below the crossbar signifies one unit. Each bead above the crossbar represents five units. Thus, the number at the far right of the abacus is nine, because one unit of five (5) touches the crossbar from the top and four single units (4) gather at the crossbar from the bottom.

The government expanded mining, ship-building, and silk making and introduced paper currency throughout the empire. The abacus—an early calculator—made its first appearance, and movable type was also invented.

In the twelfth century a nomadic group attacked the northern Song holdings, forcing the Song court to move south. As a result, the empire was divided into two parts and was ruled by Northern and Southern Song dynasties. A familiar pattern repeated itself, when court corruption and rural discontent made both dynasties ripe for overthrow by a new threat from the north—the Mongols.

Mongol Rule

A nomadic people from Mongolia, the Mongols were skilled horse riders and archers. In 1206 they had been united into one nation by their leader Genghis Khan. (A khan was the ruler of the Mongol people.) By 1215 Genghis and his troops had captured Beijing and were pushing westward to southern Russia. By 1234 the Mongols had occupied Northern Song hold-ings, and in 1276 the Southern Song capital, Hangzhou, fell to Genghis's grandson Kublai Khan.

Kublai Khan founded the Yuan dynasty and headed an extended empire, which stretched from eastern China to the Caspian Sea (near the modern Soviet Union). The Yuan dynasty was the first foreign group to rule all of China.

Under the Yuan dynasty, trade and crafts flourished, and engineers improved and extended the Grand Canal. Mathematicians invented an accurate calendar that had 365.2 days, and language experts created a new alphabet, which they could apply to all of the languages of the empire.

Marco Polo—an explorer from Venice, Italy, who visited China between 1274 and 1292—described Kublai Khan's fabulous palaces, gardens, and pavilions. The explorer's accounts astounded the courts of Europe and spurred commercial interest in China. Soon European traders and ambassadors set out for the region that Polo had named "Cathay" (China).

Despite its wealth and prestige, the empire was too vast to remain united for any length of time. In 1294, after the death of

A detail from a hand-painted European artwork depicts the Polo family (Marco is in green) kneeling before the Mongol emperor Kublai Khan. A valued aide to the emperor in the thirteenth century, Marco Polo wrote extensively of his travels in China.

The statue of a fierce, fully armed Ming warrior guards the entrance to the tombs of the Ming emperors in Beijing. By tradition, the emperors chose their burial sites and lavishly provided for their own entombments.

Kublai Khan, the realm split into four sub-regions, called khanates (realms of khans), which fought against one another.

The rivalry among the khanates weakened the Yuan dynasty. Its loss of strength allowed Zhu Yuanzhang, the leader of a secret society called the Red Turbans, to seize Nanjing (Nanking) in 1356. By 1368 he had control of the middle and lower reaches of the Chang River, and in that same year he declared himself Ming Taizu —the first ruler of the Ming dynasty.

Ming Dynasty

Between 1368 and 1644, Ming rulers governed a stable and prosperous empire. Ming Taizu's successor moved his court to Beijing, which remained the capital city until the early twentieth century. During the Ming period, royal builders constructed the Forbidden City and many of the temples in and around Beijing. In addition, the government repaired the Great Wall, much of which had crumbled away. People from newly acquired territories in the northeast and south added to China's ethnic diversity.

The royal court established trade and diplomatic relations with more than 30 countries. Ming historians recorded the visits of dignitaries from as far away as Italy and the Netherlands. The activities of Roman Catholic missionaries, who reached China in about 1600, failed to attract local interest. Moreover, the Chinese treated European diplomats and merchants as cultural inferiors.

Despite its strengths, the Ming dynasty experienced constant border disputes—particularly with the Mongols and the Japanese. During the seventeenth century, popular uprisings against the regime occurred under the leadership of a rural worker named Li Zizheng. His soldiers captured Luoyang in 1641 and set out three years later to march on Beijing. Manchurian troops, which had overthrown Ming power in the northeast beyond China's boundary, forced Li to retreat. After assassinating Li in 1645, the Manchu set up the Qing dynasty, and another foreign power ruled Chinese territory.

Qing Dynasty and Trade with the West

Unlike previous foreign rulers of China, the Manchu had adopted much of Chinese culture, including the ideals of Confucianism and the bureaucratic framework of the Ming period. As a result, the Qing dynasty enjoyed stability and expanded its territory. The population increased, and traditional livelihoods—such as agriculture and handicrafts—experienced rapid expansion.

Although the Chinese had traditionally regarded foreigners as barbarians, the Manchu established an official market in Guangzhou for foreign trade. Restrictions governed commerce with the outside world —a situation that Great Britain, a major European trading power, found unacceptable. As a result, in 1793 the British sent a messenger to the emperor Qian Long to request the opening of a British embassy in Beijing. The Chinese refused.

By the end of the eighteenth century, Qing prosperity had declined, and political corruption was rampant. Anti-Qing rebellions among the common people occurred in 1796 and lasted until 1804. These revolts greatly weakened Qing strength and gave European powers the opportunity to assert themselves in the nineteenth century.

The British were concerned that the Chinese did not want to buy British goods. The traders offered Western items in exchange for China's precious tea, silk, and porcelain. The money that the British spent

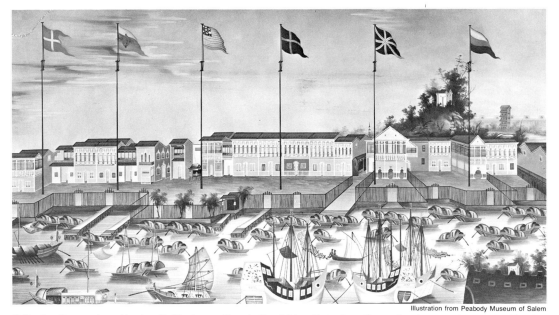

Illustration from Peabody Museum of Salem

Following the opening of trade with Western nations in the eighteenth century, Guangzhou became the center of foreign commerce. The flags of Western nations flew over the factories where traders conducted their business with Chinese merchants.

In a newspaper illustration, the Qing imperial commissioner oversees the destruction of opium-filled chests in Guangzhou. This event provoked British-Chinese opium wars in the nineteenth century. Britain wanted to trade illegal opium—an addictive drug brought to China from India—for Chinese products.

to buy China's goods was more than they earned from the sale of British commodities. As a result, Britain faced a serious trade imbalance. British merchants—helped by corrupt Chinese officials—resorted to exchanging opium (an addictive drug grown in British-held India), instead of British goods, for Chinese products.

The Chinese imperial government became alarmed by the growing addiction of its people to opium and by the outflow of silver to pay for the drug. The Qing administration appointed a special commissioner in Guangzhou to find a solution. After negotiations with the British failed to stop the opium trade, the commissioner publicly destroyed 20,000 chests of opium that had been seized from British merchants. In response, the British were determined to punish the Chinese. An opium war erupted in 1839 and lasted until the British defeated the Chinese in 1842.

Under the Treaty of Nanjing, the victorious British imposed the first of many demands on the Chinese regarding trade. Among other concessions, the British took over both the island of Hong Kong and part of the nearby Kowloon Peninsula. Subsequently, the Portuguese captured the port of Macao.

A view of the harbor at Macao appears on a nineteenth-century, lacquer-ware sewing cabinet. As a result of the opium wars, the Portuguese extended their control over the port.

Taiping Rebellion

The drain on China's silver to pay for opium grew even larger. In addition, severe famines, droughts, and floods afflicted millions of Chinese. The corrupt Qing bureaucracy did little to ease the plight of villagers, and anti-Qing movements arose. The most famous uprising was the Taiping Rebellion, which lasted from 1851 to 1864. Begun in southern China, the revolt soon spread and resulted in the deaths of as many as 30 million Chinese.

The rebellion's leaders preached the building of a free, democratic society. They wanted to abolish slavery and other social offenses and to prohibit the opium trade and gambling. The movement's followers occupied Wuhan and established a government at Nanjing. For over a decade, they ruled nearly half of China.

Intervention and Reform

Meanwhile, in areas not controlled by the rebels, foreign powers got further concessions from the Qing dynasty after a second opium war occurred in the 1850s. These new privileges included the legalization of the opium trade and the opening of more ports to foreign commerce. Because the rebellious Taiping government in Nanjing had banned opium, international powers wanted to help the Manchu eliminate the rebels. After a lengthy siege, Nanjing fell in 1864, and the conflict ended.

After the Taiping Rebellion was finally put down, the Manchu became aware of the need for internal changes. They enacted agricultural reforms, streamlined the bureaucracy, and improved schools. But these internal measures did not cure growing international troubles.

Along with trade concessions forced from the Qing dynasty, foreign powers began to take over parts of Chinese territory. The French absorbed what is now Vietnam, and the British seized Burma and enlarged Hong Kong. Following the

Courtesy of Jeannine Bayard and Kip Lilly

The Chinese empress Cixi had strong antiforeign opinions. She encouraged members of the Yi He Quan—a secret society that was also known as the Boxers—to rebel against the policies of the emperor. In 1900, as the combined imperial and Western forces put down the uprising, Cixi fled to Xi'an.

Chinese-Japanese War in 1894, the Japanese took territory in Korea as well as the island of Taiwan and the Penghus (the Pescadores).

As a result of these losses of land, outsiders controlled many of China's ports, which were opened to international commerce. Ships full of foreign goods arrived, and the vessels departed laden with Chinese tea, silk, and porcelain. Foreign trading nations competed for railway rights, naval bases, and areas of commercial influence.

As the Manchu saw their empire threatened, they enacted even more internal reforms. These changes angered the conservative ruling elite, which did not want to lose any of its power. This group covertly gave its support to the Yi He Quan—an anti-Christian, antiforeign secret society that Western nations called the Boxers. In 1900 the Boxer Rebellion erupted against the government, resulting in the deaths of many Christians and in the destruction of much of northern China. Troops from Western nations aided the Qing dynasty in putting down the uprising. In exchange for their help, foreign countries imposed further economic demands on the Manchu.

Republic of China

Despite the reforms instituted earlier by the Manchu, local anti-imperial groups flourished in the early twentieth century. In 1905 a Western-educated doctor named Sun Zhongshan (Sun Yat-sen) founded the United League. This organization was dedicated to three principles—nationalism, democracy, and social welfare. Sun's rebel movement gained momentum between 1905 and 1911 and staged many attacks on Qing power. In October 1911 imperial army troops revolted against the government and increased widespread support for the United League. In late 1911 Sun established the Republic of China in Nan-

jing and set up a temporary government, of which he was named president.

Overshadowing Sun's power, however, was Yuan Shikai—the strongest warlord in China. He took over Beijing before Sun could establish a permanent government and forced Pu Yi, the last Chinese emperor, to resign. Yuan named himself provisional president of China. As Yuan expanded his power, Sun's support declined. In 1913 Sun fled to Japan, and Yuan, with the help of other warlords, unsuccessfully attempted to establish himself as emperor.

Guomindang and Communist Movements

Following World War I (1914–1918), the victorious anti-German powers awarded Chinese territory to Japan as compensation for Japan's naval maneuvers against Germany during the conflict. Popular demonstrations against the land losses occurred on May 4, 1919. Sun, who had

Independent Picture Service

The first cabinet of the Republic of China included Sun Zhongshan (Sun Yat-sen, *second from right in front row*). In the early 1900s, he founded the United League—one of several anti-imperial organizations.

Independent Picture Service

Sun's greatest rival for power was Yuan Shikai *(center)*, a military commander of northern China. Yuan declared himself president of the republic in 1912, and Sun fled to Japan the following year.

Courtesy of Woodrow Parks

Sun Zhongshan is still honored as the father of modern China. His Guomindang (Kuomintang) movement was modeled after the Soviet Communist party, which helped him to regain power in China in 1923.

Photo by UPI/Bettmann Newsphotos

After Sun died in 1925, Jiang Jieshi (Chiang Kai-shek), one of Sun's deputies in the Guomindang, took over the party's leadership. Disagreements with the Chinese Communists led Jiang to break with them in 1927, setting up a conflict that lasted for over two decades.

returned from Japan in 1916, took advantage of these antigovernment sentiments. His activities built widespread support for his new Guomindang (Kuomintang) movement, or Nationalist party, which had evolved from the United League. In addition to local aid, Sun sought international help. Spurned by Western nations, he asked the Soviet Union for assistance and found willing listeners.

Meanwhile, a member of the May Fourth movement—named after the earlier demonstration—founded the Chinese Communist party (CCP) in 1921. The party sought to expand its base of support in order to become a national organization. By 1923 Sun Zhongshan was convinced that victory over the warlords lay in joining forces with the Communists. Thereafter, the Guomindang admitted Communists to its membership and set up a military academy near Guangzhou. A young, Soviet-trained officer named Jiang Jieshi (Chiang Kai-shek) became president of the academy,

and the Communist leader Zhou Enlai served as dean of studies.

When Sun Zhongshan died in 1925, Jiang Jieshi followed him as leader of the Guomindang. With the Communists, Jiang brought southern China under control, established a government at Wuhan, and took Shanghai. Soon afterward, he—as well as the other members of his party—decided to break with the Communists.

After staging a coup within the Guomindang, Jiang established a national government at Nanjing in 1927, and the Wuhan administration collapsed. Within a year, Beijing—the center of warlord activity—agreed to come under Jiang's authority. Western powers and foreign banking institutions recognized Jiang's government, giving it international legitimacy.

The 1930s

Despite its severely weakened position, the CCP did not fall apart. It organized an

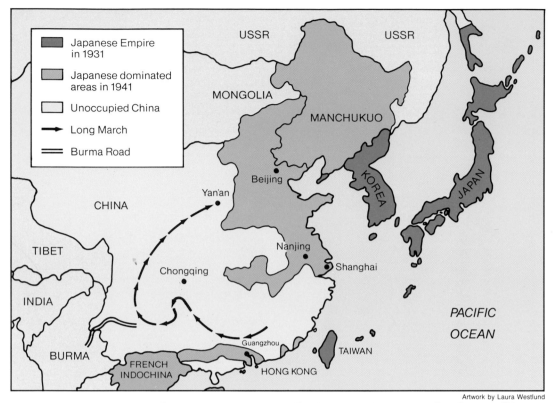

Artwork by Laura Westlund

Two wars were happening within China in the 1930s and 1940s. The Japanese took over parts of northeastern China—an area they called Manchukuo—as well as regions around Beijing, Nanjing, and Shanghai. At the same time, Jiang's army pursued the Chinese Communist forces in central China—an operation that resulted in the Long March.

uprising in the province of Hunan. The revolt was one of several that were intended to disrupt the new Nationalist government. Led by a young villager named Mao Zedong, the rural rebellion fueled the public's anti-Jiang feelings. The two opposing sides—Nationalists and Communists— were ready for conflict.

The Communists attempted to set up a rival government in southern China, and Jiang became determined to break their power and numbers. His forces attempted to blockade the Red (Communist) Army, which broke through government lines and began the Long March in 1934. This exhausting, year-long trek covered over 6,000 miles of nearly inaccessible mountains and crossed some of China's mightiest rivers. In 1935 only a few thousand of the original 300,000 Red soldiers survived

the walk to the northern province of Shaanxi. During the march, CCP members chose Mao Zedong as leader of the party.

Wherever the Red Army went, it instituted land reforms, drove out land lords, and established equal rights for women. The soldiers tried to create a society that was based on law and order. The Nationalist armies, on the other hand, became known for their corruption and for their poor military training.

The Communists were not Jiang's only enemies, however. Throughout the 1930s, the Japanese—in search of land and raw materials—had seized territory in northern China and along the coast. At first, Jiang's government was more concerned about the Communists than about the Japanese. But Jiang feared that the CCP would turn the widespread national anger over the Japa-

Independent Picture Service

nese land seizures against his government. Indeed, in 1936 Jiang's own Nationalist troops kidnapped him and forced him to sign an alliance with the CCP to evict the invaders.

World War II and Its Aftermath

When the Asian phase of World War II broke out in 1941, China had been at war with Japan for four years. As a result, China joined the allied Western powers against Japan, Italy, and Nazi Germany.

Independent Picture Service

In the 1940s Japanese troops marched along the Great Wall of China *(above)* as soldiers of the Communist Red Army led by Mao Zedong fought the Japanese from this same historic landmark *(right).*

Independent Picture Service

Mao built his grass-roots support among rural workers and urban dwellers. Here, he chats with farmers in Yan'an, the site of his Red Army headquarters in Shaanxi province.

Within China, Communist guerrilla bands in the north showed the most active resistance to the Japanese—who had by now occupied Beijing, Shanghai, Nanjing, and Guangzhou. During the remainder of the war, Jiang accepted all the Western aid he could get by way of the Burma Road and India. After the surrender of Japan in 1945, Jiang—with U.S. backing—succeeded in taking over many cities in northern China.

But Jiang and his supporters had underestimated CCP strength, which had increased during the war. They also had not taken into account the appeal of Communist ideas to millions of rural and urban workers. The CCP's well-organized propaganda attracted the Chinese masses and left the Nationalists in a weakened political position.

Neither side felt that it could cooperate with its opponent, and full-scale civil war erupted between the Communists and the Nationalists in mid-1946. By the end of 1948 the Red Army had driven Nationalist forces out of northeastern China. In January 1949 Beijing fell without a struggle.

The People's Liberation Army (PLA), as the Red Army came to be called, reached the Chang River. By the autumn of 1949 all of China, except for Xizang, had been occupied. (The PLA invaded Xizang in 1950 and had fully subdued it by 1959.) Mao Zedong declared the formation of the People's Republic of China (PRC) in Beijing. In late 1949 Jiang and some of his supporters fled to Taiwan, where they relocated the Nationalist government.

People's Republic of China

Under Mao Zedong, the old order, which had existed for thousands of years, was abolished. Mao's longtime supporter Zhou Enlai had authority over government ministries, and he began to nationalize (change

The design of China's flag was adopted in 1949, when Mao established the People's Republic of China (PRC). Red stands for the revolution, although the color has also been symbolic of the Chinese people. The large star represents Communism, and the four smaller stars signify the four national groups of workers.

At Tian'anmen Square in Beijing, a large sculpture depicts events in the Chinese revolution that resulted in the founding of the PRC.

from private to state ownership) land, industry, banking, and commercial operations during the 1950s. Financial support from the Soviet Union helped to bolster the new regime, which set in motion five-year plans to revitalize the Chinese economy.

The PRC's close relationship with the Soviet Union also led to some joint military operations in the 1950s. Both nations sent aid, weapons, and soldiers to help the Communist North Koreans in their attempt to reunite Korea, which had been divided into two parts after World War II. Under the banner of the United Nations (UN), Western countries fought alongside the South Koreans. Nearly one million Chinese died in the Korean War, which lasted from 1950 to 1953.

In 1958 Mao introduced the Great Leap Forward—a set of ideas designed to make China economically self-sufficient by reversing some of the policies of the early 1950s. The government expanded industry and gave incentives to develop local manufacturing centers. Agriculture was organized into communes—a form of group farming. Although most acreages were small, as many as 50,000 people lived on a single commune. New laws divided the labor force into brigades to maximize productivity. The profit motive (working for personal gain) disappeared, and the idea that all labor and all wages were equal took the place of individual incentives.

Despite its broad vision of improving China, the Great Leap Forward failed. In fact, it led not only to a decline in industrial output but also to drops in food production, which caused the starvation of millions of people from 1958 to 1962. The economy returned to more moderate socialist policies after 1962.

The 1960s

In the early 1960s China's relations with the Soviet Union severely deteriorated. Critical of Soviet attempts to coexist with the West, China believed itself to be the guardian of pure Communist ideals and saw war with the West as inevitable. In 1960 the Soviet Union stopped sending technical aid to China, and in 1962 the Soviets did not support China in its border war with India. Relations between the two huge Communist powers sank to their lowest point in the mid-1960s.

In 1965 Mao generated another radical change called the Great Proletarian Cultural Revolution, which was designed to combat bureaucratic slowness and to foster pure Communist ideals. The cultural revolution was actually the result of one branch of the government—led by Mao—conflicting with another branch of the

35

During the 1960s and 1970s, Chinese support for followers of Mao swung wildly. Members of the army *(left)* enthusiastically denounced Deng Xiaoping in 1976, when he was relieved of all power in the Chinese Communist party (CCP). Later that year, however, Deng regained his rank and authority in Chinese politics. Soldiers *(below)* showed their support for Deng's efforts to weaken a political faction—including Mao's widow—that tried to remain in power after Mao's death in 1976.

government, under the control of Liu Shaoqi. Mao distrusted the antisocialist trends in the government, while his opponents—including Liu and Deng Xiaoping—advocated less ideological and more practical approaches to running the country. Nevertheless, the cultural revolution had nationwide effects.

Inspired by Mao's ideas, Chinese students—called Red Guards—attacked much of traditional Chinese society, including individuals who had previously had contacts with the Nationalist government and people who had relatives in other countries. Most universities in China were closed, and Mao urged the students to learn from the peasants by living in com-

munes. Red Guards publicly humiliated teachers and skilled managers, who were sent to communes as a form of punishment. As many as 100 million people died or served time in hard-labor camps during this period of national upheaval.

Internal Struggles

By the late 1960s the Chinese felt the long-term negative effects of the cultural revolution, especially in the areas of planning and education. By 1969 two political views had emerged to deal with the nation's growing economic and social problems. Each standpoint was championed by a leader close to Mao. Lin Biao, Mao's presumed

Zhou Enlai *(seated in front of the window)* — **seen here in conversation with workers in Shanxi province** — **steered China toward a foreign policy that included relations with Western nations.**

successor, favored a closer relationship with the Soviet Union. Zhou Enlai advocated a more moderate approach, which would include contacts with the West.

Lin Biao died in an airplane crash in 1971, and his death weakened support for his political stance. In the same year the United Nations recognized the People's Republic of China as the legitimate government of China, and the PRC replaced Taiwan as China's representative in the UN.

China also improved its relations with Western nations. In 1972—in a dramatic reversal of U.S. policy, which had long supported the Nationalists on Taiwan as the rightful government of China—U.S. president Richard Nixon visited China. Trade and tourism between China and the United States slowly developed after the visit. The two nations restored full diplomatic relations in early 1979.

China's improved relationship with the United States and its continuing poor

In 1972 Chinese leaders met with U.S. president Richard Nixon. This contact symbolized U.S. acceptance of the PRC as China's government. Until 1972, the United States had steadfastly named the Nationalist regime on Taiwan as the rightful ruler of China.

Courtesy of Jeannine Bayard and Kip Lilly

relationship with the Soviet Union signaled the end of the cultural revolution. Although Zhou Enlai's view had prevailed, his position in the Chinese leadership was not secure until after the death of Mao Zedong on September 9, 1976.

After Zhou also died in late 1976, a power struggle preceded elections within the CCP leadership to fill the positions that Mao and Zhou had held. Party members chose Hua Guofeng—who had ties to both Maoists and moderates—as chairman of the CCP. Deng Xiaoping—a supporter of Zhou Enlai—became vice premier, vice chairman of the CCP, and chief of staff of the army. After the elections, Mao's widow, Jiang Qing, was arrested because she had tried to retain power along with three other Maoists (together called "the Gang of Four"). The trial of these politicians led to the decline of Maoist influence on Chinese affairs at high levels.

Reconstructing China

Following the party elections, Deng gained influence, and Hua's role became weaker. By 1980 Deng had become China's leader, and he aimed to invigorate the Chinese leadership with young, educated Communists. Many longtime and highly placed supporters of Mao were convicted of corruption, and people from midlevel positions in the party replaced them.

In addition to bureaucratic innovations, Deng introduced the Four Modernizations

Plan, which promoted new developments and productivity in the areas of agriculture, industry, national defense, and science and technology. This program coincided with the growth of economic relations with Japan and the United States.

Old and New Issues

Despite China's change in direction, continuing conflicts and new problems surfaced in the late 1980s. Attention again focused on the Autonomous Region of Xizang. In 1950—when the region was still known as Tibet—the Chinese had invaded. Frequent uprisings occurred in the 1950s as the Tibetans resisted full integration into Chinese culture. In the late 1980s, Xizang experienced religious unrest in Lhasa, the capital of the autonomous region. In this historic city, demonstrating

Buddhist monks clashed with Chinese police. Similar riots erupted in other towns in the area, as local groups in Xizang pushed for independence.

A new problem in China—student unrest—also became apparent in the late 1980s. Chinese university students in Shanghai, Beijing, and Tianjin began to demonstrate for improved living and working conditions—benefits that foreign undergraduates in China already enjoyed. Eventually, the protests expanded to include calls for greater political freedom.

In mid-1989, students began to demonstrate in favor of democratic reform and for the end of political corruption. Their gatherings—which took place for several weeks in Beijing's Tian'anmen Square—became the focus of international interest as the number of workers and students swelled to the hundreds of thousands. In

One of the intentions of Deng Xiaoping's Four Modernizations Plan has been to bring new technology to the agricultural sector. Here, farmers use a foot-operated device to irrigate their land.

Students carry a sign reading "News Freedom" during demonstrations in Shanghai in 1987. In 1989 students again protested governmental limitations on their rights. Both student actions resulted in changes in the CCP leadership. Unlike the earlier demonstrations, however, the events of the spring of 1989 ended in violence. Troops fired on the demonstrators, and later some of the protest's leaders were executed.

Photo by Reuters/Bettmann Newsphotos

June the government sent troops to the area with orders to end the demonstration. Violence erupted between the soldiers and the protesters, with hundreds killed and thousands wounded in a one-sided conflict.

Following the unrest in Tian'anmen Square, power shifts occurred in the Chinese government. Conservative leaders seized authority within the CCP from liberal and moderate politicians. As of early 1990, major policy decisions still required the approval of the aging Deng Xiaoping, although he increasingly handed over official jobs to his younger supporters. It re-

Deng Xiaoping, aged 86 in 1990, has been China's undisputed leader since 1980. His efforts to modernize China have led to fewer restrictions on trade. In recent years, he has gradually turned over his CCP posts to his younger colleagues.

Photo by UPI/Bettmann Newsphotos

mains to be seen if the recent tensions in China will affect economic policies or contacts with the West.

Younger leaders and continued economic expansion are major goals on the government's agenda. Yet inflation and the nation's increasing population—despite strict family-planning procedures—threaten to undermine China's attempts to achieve economic growth.

Government

The Constitution of 1978 identifies the National People's Congress as the most important legislative organization in China. The CCP overwhelmingly dominates the elected membership of the congress. Since the congress is too large to be an effective instrument of daily policy, a standing committee of 79 members exercises power in the name of the congress.

To handle the day-to-day duties of national administration, the congress elects a state council, which consists of the premier and various ministers. Its members come from the most powerful ranks of the CCP and often hold important posts in the party. As a result, the state council reflects the party's stance on most issues.

The highest judicial power belongs to a supreme people's court, which ensures that the policies of the CCP are enforced. This court also supervises the activities of lower courts, which people's tribunals supplement at the local level.

For administrative purposes, China is divided into 23 provinces, 5 autonomous regions, and 3 independent urban areas. (The PRC counts Taiwan as a province of China, although the island maintains its own administration under the Nationalist government.)

The autonomous regions have a high level of self-rule, especially in the realm of culture. This policy reflects the government's acceptance of non-Chinese groups—called national minorities—that live in the PRC. These subdivisions are Xizang, Ningxia, Nei Monggol, Xinjiang, and Guangxi. Approximately 70 million members of national minorities live in these autonomous areas.

The self-governing municipalities are Beijing, Shanghai, and Tianjin. Independent administrations run these cities and report directly to the central government.

Courtesy of Mark Anderson

The main assembly room of Beijing's Great Hall of the People, where the CCP gathers, can hold 10,000 people.

The children of factory workers in Beijing play with toys at a state-run kindergarten. Most Chinese work, and day care begins at an early age.

3) The People

Most of China's 1.1 billion inhabitants live in the fertile, eastern one-third of the country. Throughout China, the standard of living is steadily rising, and in the 1980s increasing numbers of families could buy televisions, radios, bicycles, refrigerators, sewing machines, and other items that were once considered luxuries.

The position and rights of women also have improved. Before the revolution, fathers could sell their daughters into marriage, and husbands could force their wives into prostitution. Now Chinese women work in government and industry and are members of the armed forces. Nevertheless, cultural prejudices still operate, and many skilled women advance slowly in their professions compared to men with similiar qualifications and training.

Ninety-three percent of the population are of Mongolian ancestry and are called Han, or ethnic Chinese. Although the Han share social and cultural traits and use the same written form of Chinese, regional differences occur within this group. Spoken languages, for example, may distinguish a southerner from a northerner, and livelihoods may differ from west to east.

National Minorities

In addition to the Han, there are over 50 other ethnic groups in China. The government recognizes these communities as national minorities, since together they make up only 7 percent of the population. In general, the national minorities are concentrated in the autonomous regions near China's borders. As a result, the groups often have ethnic ties with peoples in neighboring countries.

The government permits national minorities some cultural independence, and, if their numbers are large, they have a greater level of political self-rule. Minorities are allowed to study their own language as well as Mandarin Chinese—the official language of China. In addition, minorities are not subject to the government's One Family–One Child policy, which limits population growth among the Han.

China's 12 million Zhuang, who generally live in Guangxi (a southern autonomous region), are ethnically related to the people of Thailand and constitute the largest national minority. The Hui, with over six million members, are Chinese-speaking Muslims (followers of the Islamic religion). They dwell in Ningxia, Gansu, and Qinghai in north central China and make their livings by herding livestock.

The nation's third largest minority—the Turkic-speaking Uighur—inhabit the deserts of Xinjiang and raise animals and cultivate crops near oases (fertile areas). They

Under the PRC, women have broader job options than they had under previous regimes. These pilots are part of China's air force.

Tibetan monks—members of one of China's national minorities—engage in religious discussions at a monastery in Qinghai.

43

have language affiliations with peoples in bordering parts of the Soviet Union. Other national minorities include the Yi, the Mongols, the Miao, and the Kazaks.

Perhaps the most distinctly non-Chinese minority are the Tibetans, who reside in the highlands of Xizang and in Qinghai (a west central autonomous region). They make their livings as farmers and herders. Tibetans follow Lamaistic Buddhism, a religion that is a mixture of traditional Buddhism and local beliefs.

Language and Literature

Instead of a lettered alphabet, the Chinese language uses symbols called ideograms, which represent ideas or concepts, rather than sounds. There are thousands of ideograms, and memorization is the main way to learn this written form. A person must know approximately 5,000 symbols in order to read a newspaper.

China's ability to educate its population is complicated by the large number of ideograms that a student must memorize in

Courtesy of Woodrow Parks

This dancer is among the more than two million Mongols who inhabit regions in northern China.

order to advance in education. Chinese writing has been simplified somewhat, however. A phonetic alphabet—called *pinyin*—which spells words with Latin letters, enables the Chinese to use Western typewriters and computers.

Courtesy of Woodrow Parks

The complexities of the Chinese language present a challenge to this young woman using a Chinese typewriter.

A sign in Hangzhou shows a few of the characters that form the Chinese written language. These columns are read vertically, beginning at the top righthand side.

Perhaps the most widely read of all Chinese classical literature are the *Five Classics,* which the philosopher Confucius wrote in the sixth century B.C. These writings contain the key political and ethical concepts of Confucianism.

The Tang period (618–907) was the golden age of Chinese poetry. The most distinguished writers of this period were Li Bo, Du Fu, and Bo Juyi. They produced satiric verse, beautiful ballads, and political poetry. The Ming dynasty (1368–1644) was the age of the novel. *The Romance of the Three Kingdoms,* attributed to the writer Luo Guanzhong, recounts the activities of rival warlords during the centuries that followed the fall of the Han family of rulers.

The end of the nineteenth century brought new literary themes, which described China's loss of dignity at the hands of Western powers. Kang Youwei wrote about the suffering of China, the problems of racism, and inequality—especially of women.

One of China's greatest writers in the early twentieth century was Lu Xun, who used classical forms of Chinese poetry and filled them with images of nationalism. In his short stories, Lu described the effects of poverty, superstition, and human suffering on China.

People who want to read at an outdoor library in Changsha, the capital of Hunan province, pay the equivalent of 10 cents to study the entire day.

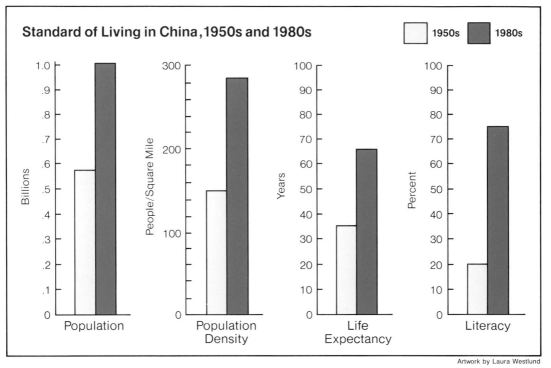

Standard of Living in China, 1950s and 1980s

☐ 1950s ■ 1980s

Population (Billions)

Population Density (People/Square Mile)

Life Expectancy (Years)

Literacy (Percent)

Artwork by Laura Westlund

Statistics from the 1950s and the 1980s compare the standard of living in China over a nearly 40-year span. (Data provided by the Population Reference Bureau and the Embassy of the People's Republic of China.)

After 1949, the PRC ordered all authors to write stories that praised the new state. Writers who did not follow this guideline did not get their books published in the country. The most widely read works in the 1960s and 1970s were those of Mao Zedong. Since 1977, however, writers have returned to traditional Chinese styles and to Western literary themes.

Health

China experienced an immense population explosion in the 1960s and 1970s. As a result, the Chinese government introduced a birth control program during the 1980s for the Han, but not for members of the national minorities. This policy prohibits ethnic Chinese families from having more than one child.

Families that have more than one offspring are penalized by having their wages reduced, by risking job demotions, and by

Courtesy of Steve Feinstein

A poster advocates the One Family–One Child policy that is designed to limit China's population growth.

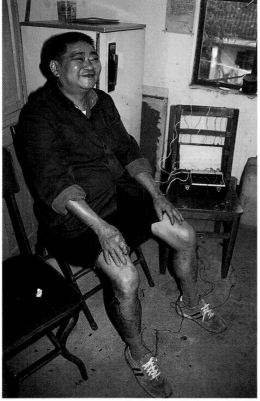

This man is undergoing acupuncture—an ancient medical treatment accepted throughout China—in a clinic near Shanghai. Needles inserted at specific points in his legs relieve the pain in his knees.

Courtesy of Jeannine Bayard and Kip Lilly

facing the criticism of their neighbors. The birth control program has been more successful in China's cities than in the countryside. In rural areas, many people still believe that they must have several children to help to farm the land.

Since the establishment of the PRC in 1949, the state has taken care of the elderly, the sick, and the disabled. Improvements in sanitation facilities and in the availability of modern medical care have raised the life expectancy figure for the Chinese to 66 years—higher than the average of 62 for Asia. The nation's infant mortality rate is 44 deaths in every 1,000 live births. This statistic is good when compared to Asia's average of 78 deaths per 1,000.

In addition to Western medical techniques, the Chinese support traditional

In Suzhou, eastern China, an illustrated sign describes the health hazards of smoking.

Courtesy of Mark Anderson

methods for curing illness. Special herbs and attention to nutrition are regarded as alternatives to modern drugs. Acupuncture is one of China's oldest forms of treatment. This ancient technique involves the insertion of needles at pressure points in the body to relieve pain and to cure disease. Since the 1950s, acupuncturists have used the procedure to numb patients who are about to have surgery.

Education

At the beginning of the twentieth century, only 15 percent of the Chinese could read and write. After the PRC came to power in 1949, the educational system changed radically. Primary education became available for all children, and adult education programs were aimed at increasing literacy among China's older population. In the late 1980s, 75 percent of China's population over the age of 12 were literate.

Differences exist between rural and urban educational facilities, and the number of qualified teachers is too low for the number of school-aged Chinese. In general, however, Chinese children attend elementary school between the ages of 6 and 12. They study geography, history, mathematics, natural science, and physical education. Middle (secondary) school lasts for three years and includes vocational and technical courses. Foreign languages—including English—are an important part of the coursework at the middle level.

During the cultural revolution in the 1960s, the government closed the universities. Nearly an entire generation of Chinese youth had no access to either higher education or the latest technologies. As a result, university education has become a priority for China in recent times, but the number of openings is low, and the number of applicants is high. University entrance exams are difficult, and only 1 percent of

Courtesy of Steve Feinstein

At a middle school in Guilin, northeastern Guangxi, students exercise their eyes as part of their morning classwork.

Courtesy of Mark Anderson

Lingyin Temple—a Buddhist site in Hangzhou—features religious rock carvings dating from about a thousand years ago.

Courtesy of Library of Congress

Born in Shandong province in the sixth century B.C., Confucius formulated strict notions of morality and social responsibility. These ideals guided official policies of Chinese governments for 2,000 years. Followers of Confucius spread his teachings to Japan, Korea, and Vietnam.

high school graduates get into postsecondary institutions. In addition, educational facilities have not kept pace with population growth. Dormitories are crowded, and school meals are inadequate. Some of the student demonstrations in the late 1980s were directed against these shortages within the university system.

Religion

Because of its commitment to solving problems through science and politics, the Communist government discourages the practice of religion in China. Nevertheless, religious believers may follow their faiths as long as they do not seek to convert others. Christian missions—a significant force in China's history in the late nineteenth and early twentieth centuries—no longer operate in China. Since the early 1980s, however, the government has allowed some Christian churches to reopen.

The three main religions of ancient China were Confucianism, Buddhism, and Dao-

ism. Over the centuries, some Chinese have combined various elements of these faiths.

Buddhism, introduced from India, is based on the teachings of Gautama Buddha, a prince who lived in India in the sixth century B.C. He gave up a life of luxury to seek divine knowledge. Lamaistic Buddhism—followed by the people in Xizang—derives from Buddhism but has also adopted traditional beliefs long held by local people. During the cultural revolution of the 1950s and 1960s, monks in Xizang were arrested, and the Chinese army destroyed many religious buildings. Nevertheless, the Tibetans have retained their religion, and it continues to be a unifying force in their culture.

Founded by Confucius in the sixth century B.C., Confucianism is a code of ethics rather than a set of rituals. The ideals of Confucius strongly influenced Chinese society for 2,000 years. Confucianism stresses moral standards and encourages society to be strictly arranged into classes.

49

During the imperial era, elaborate ceremonies accompanied the arrival of the emperor at the Hall of Prayer. Here, the royal leader would pray for good harvests and perform other religious rituals. The roof of the fifteenth-century structure is made of 50,000 blue-glazed tiles over an interlaced wooden frame.

This factor made Confucianism an unpopular philosophy after 1949, when the government emphasized equality. For Confucians, parents have authority over their children, men rule women, and the educated classes govern the workers. Reverence for one's ancestors is also a key element of Confucianism.

Daoism—which developed in the fourth century B.C. as a response to the strictness of Confucianism—is based on *Dao De Jing* (The Classic of the Way and the Virtue). These writings encourage a lifestyle that is in harmony with nature and that avoids social stresses and duties.

The Islamic religion, founded by the prophet Muhammad in Arabia in the seventh century A.D., also has supporters in China. Although government figures are scarce, estimates indicate that at least 2

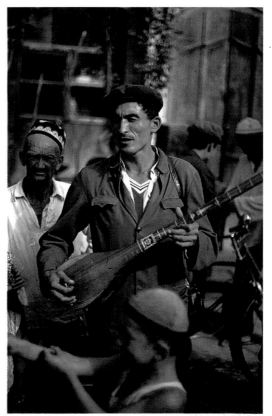

A wandering minstrel in western Xinjiang plays a traditional Chinese musical instrument.

percent of the Chinese are Muslims. Most of the religion's followers are Hui who live near Mongolian areas that have historical ties to Islamic nations farther west.

The Arts

Chinese music uses a five-tone scale—as opposed to the eight-tone pattern characteristic of Western music. Chinese folk music may be played on a *qin* (a seven-stringed lute), a *san xian* (a three-stringed, guitarlike instrument), or a *suo na* (a horn). Various gongs, drums, and flutes also appear among Chinese musical instruments. Some Chinese rock musicians have developed their own style, which has been influenced by groups that perform in Hong Kong and on Taiwan.

Chinese watercolor paintings first were done on pottery and silk but have since become common on paper. Natural landscape images, such as waterfalls or mountains, were popular during China's imperial era. Painters also depicted officials of the Chinese court, as well as the emperors themselves.

Courtesy of Freer Gallery of Art, Smithsonian Institution, Washington, D.C.

Pottery is among China's most famous arts. This example is from the Ming period (1368–1644), when porcelain design reached an artistic height.

Calligraphy (elaborate hand-lettering) is often a vital element in Chinese paintings. A precise and exacting art, calligraphy has been popular throughout China's past, and elegantly penned poems often appear alone or on painted artworks.

Imperial patronage funded many of China's artworks. Empress Cixi commissioned this marble boat. She used money intended for the imperial navy to pay for the boat's construction.

Courtesy of Mark Anderson

Courtesy of Woodrow Parks

The work of Wang Ge Yi, a modern painter living in Shanghai, calls to mind the traditions of Chinese landscape painting.

Although Chinese pottery has a long history, the period of the Ming dynasty (1368–1644) was a time of special excellence in decorative arts. Red-and-black lacquered boxes and delicate blue-and-white ceramics became trademarks of this creative period in imperial China. Indeed, Chinese porcelain was among the most important trade items exchanged with the West in the eighteenth and nineteenth centuries.

Modern art began in China at the turn of the twentieth century, when national themes moved away from tradition and toward methods that dramatized current events. Li Hua, for example, is famous for his woodcuts, which depicted the exploitation of the Chinese by foreigners.

After the establishment of the PRC, the Communist government adopted a political ideology for art, called Socialist Realism. Works had to be realistic in form but also had to illustrate socialist themes, such as the achievements of the people and the building of socialism. In the 1980s Chinese artists mixed traditional Chinese techniques and Western approaches.

Courtesy of Carl Wilcox

A Ming-era marble stairway ornamented with dragons and clouds leads to a temple in the Forbidden City.

52

Food

Chinese cuisine is popular throughout the world, and the Chinese eat many foods—including shark fins, bird's-nest soup, slugs, frogs, jellyfish, and seaweed—that are unfamiliar to Western diners. Pork and fowl are far more common than lamb or beef. These preferences are linked to the lack of grazing land near populated areas and to insufficient feed to raise sheep and cows.

The Chinese have a special way of cooking—called stir-frying—in which meat and vegetables are quickly stirred in hot oil in a round pan called a wok. The Chinese use chopsticks—slender wooden rods—to eat their meals. Eggs, noodles, bean curd, and rice—mixed with tasty sauces—make up the balance of an ordinary Chinese meal. Common beverages are tea and beer, with rice wine available for ceremonial occasions.

The foods eaten in China differ from region to region. The best-known regional cuisines are from Guangdong, Sichuan, and Hunan provinces. Despite the many styles of Chinese food preparation, the diet of the average Chinese consists mainly of vegetables and rice or noodles. Meat is considered a luxury. Furthermore, estimates suggest that as much as 10 percent of the Chinese population, particularly in small towns and less industrialized areas, suffer from malnutrition.

Using chopsticks, patrons at a Nanjing restaurant eat their lunch.

Courtesy of Woodrow Parks

Courtesy of Mark Anderson

A market in Wanxian offers dried squid for sale.

Courtesy of F. Mattioli/FAO

Women field-workers pick a salad green called chicken feather that has been sown among cabbage plants. The laborers work outside Shanghai on a commune, or township, that produces 200 to 300 tons of vegetables each day.

4) The Economy

After the PRC was established in 1949, its five-year plans focused on economic development as well as on modernization of the agricultural sector. The government nationalized farms, industries, and businesses and built railways and roads. New laws combined farmland into collective units called communes, and economic planning programs gave industry special attention.

Political upheavals since 1949 have hampered steady economic growth in China. The regime continued to focus on modernization in the late 1980s, however. A blend of socialist ideals and personal incentives has increased production in many sectors of the economy. Nevertheless, providing China's large population with enough food remains the country's biggest economic challenge in the 1990s.

Agriculture

Farming is the livelihood of 90 percent of China's people. Eleven percent of the nation's territory is under cultivation, and only a small proportion of that amount is farmed with the aid of machinery. Buffalo, horses, donkeys, and mules are much more commonly used than tractors are. Furthermore, little land can be spared for the cultivation of fodder crops, so that there is limited livestock raising. Pigs and poultry are kept because they can find their own food.

COMMUNES

After 1949 China underwent a series of complex reforms in landownership and use. The first reform was the establishment of agricultural cooperatives. The government pooled land and financial resources and paid wages—mostly in the form of food—to the cooperatives' members after the crops were harvested. The revenues made by the cooperatives, however, were not enough to fund large-scale farming.

Under Mao's Great Leap Forward, the government combined the cooperatives into larger units, called people's communes. These groupings were then subdivided into smaller units called production teams and work brigades. By the 1980s, about half of China's one billion people lived on communes.

When Deng Xiaoping became the leader of China, he reexamined the efficiency of the commune system and decided it needed to be updated. As a result, the government has gradually abandoned the communes in favor of a system based on greater individual economic reward.

New laws have allowed households or individuals to farm communal land for their own needs. Rural workers have eagerly accepted this principle, and production in all areas has risen dramatically. The new policy has led to the development of a broad network of privately owned markets as production of food has increased.

CROPS

China has two main crop-producing regions—northeastern China and southeastern China—which are roughly divided by the Qin Range. Drier than the semitropical southeast, northeastern China produces most of the country's wheat, although local farmers also plant corn, cotton, and sorghum. Soil conservation, protection

Photo by Ruthi Soudack

Fewer planting restrictions in the 1980s enabled farmers to grow extra food for sale in local markets. Here, surplus goods—such as eggplants, cucumbers, and Brussels sprouts—are sold at local prices in Kunming, the capital of Yunnan province.

Courtesy of Steve Feinstein

The fertile soil of Hunan province receives plentiful rainfall, and farmers carefully tend their fields to attain large crop yields.

55

Paddies full of rice plants spill down the hillsides of Hunan. The south's long growing season and farmers' skillful use of limited cropland have helped to make China nearly self-sufficient in food production in the 1980s.

Workers at a fish-breeding farm near Shanghai harvest a catch of fresh-water fish.

from flooding, and good irrigation techniques have improved the northeast's ability to cultivate food crops. Yet its climate can be severe, and its short growing season hampers production levels.

In contrast, southeastern China receives plenty of rain, has a milder climate, and enjoys a long growing season. Rice farming predominates, and farmers are able to harvest two—and sometimes three—crops of rice from the same land in a year. The region also produces potatoes, cotton, and tea. Chemical fertilizers have improved the region's soil, which has a high acid content, and crop yields are usually large.

China is also a substantial producer of tobacco, pears, apples, melons, carrots, and cabbages. Farmers in the Shandong Peninsula grow peanuts, and those on Hainan Island plant tropical crops, such as bananas and pineapples.

Fishing and Forestry

The coastal provinces of China support an expanding fishing industry, which became more mechanized in the 1980s. Bigger boats are able to go farther out to sea for longer periods of time. Fishing is also intensive in the large deltas of the Huang, Chang, and Zhu rivers and in the nation's streams and canals. Fishermen catch approximately five million tons of fish and shellfish each year.

Fishery workers raise four different kinds of carp—one of China's main sources of protein—in specially prepared ponds. Enclosed in bamboo frames, grass carp feed on grass and leaves, which float on the water. Big-headed carp and silver carp eat plankton—tiny animal and plant life contained in the water and in the silt at the bottom of the pond. Common carp feed on almost anything. In ground-up form, carp

In Guangxi, laborers load bamboo logs on trucks. A program of reforestation, as well as the fast-growing nature of the plants, protects bamboo from extinction in China's dwindling wooded areas.

have also become a valuable source of fertilizer.

Much of China's populated and fertile land has been cleared of trees, leaving only 13 percent of China forested. The country's woodlands are concentrated in the northwest and southwest and in border areas, where there are few farms and settlements.

Although in short supply, wood provides raw material for the construction and paper industries. The government has begun a program of afforestation—that is, of turning open land into forests. The success of the new plan is visible around several of China's large cities.

Mining and Industry

China is rich in minerals that are only now beginning to be mined. Abundant coal deposits, chiefly in the north and northeast, have fueled industry for decades. The Nan

Courtesy of Steve Feinstein

Using a hand-held tool, a carpenter cuts a log at Xi'an to repair the old city walls.

Courtesy of National Supply Company

A platform in the Bo Sea off China's eastern coast can plunge its drill as deep as 20,000 feet in search of oil.

Range, the Yungui Plateau, the Tian Mountains, and the Qin Range hold vast reserves of lead, zinc, copper, and tungsten (a heat-resistant mineral).

The Chinese discovered oil in Xinjiang and Gansu, as well as in the waters off the eastern coast in the early 1960s. As a result, China is a major oil producer and is able to satisfy some of its energy needs with its own petroleum products. On China's northern border, miners extract gold, and they exploit uranium deposits in both Sichuan and Xinjiang.

The world's largest supplies of antimony —a metal that forms numerous useful alloys with other metals—are located in Hunan. Iron ore has become a major mining item, and large, low-grade deposits ex-

A 75-horsepower tractor nears the end of the production line at the Red Tractor Factory in Luoyang. The plant employs about 50,000 people, all of whom live within its boundaries. Housing, schools, shops, and medical facilities are part of the complex.

ist in the northeast. With these reserves, the government has been able to expand the nation's iron and steel industries.

After 1949 the government gave much attention to building factories in many parts of the country and to modernizing existing plants. In the 1980s facilities in Shenyang produced heavy machinery and track for China's railway system. Anshan —one of China's three major iron and steel bases—manufactures 100,000 tons of steel pipes each year. A jointly owned U.S.-Chinese auto plant opened in Shanghai in the mid-1980s.

Because northern China is rich in coal deposits, the country continues to produce steam locomotives that use coal as fuel. Here, a new model with its red cowcatcher (metal grate) rolls off the assembly line at Datong.

Although the cities of Shanghai and Tianjin still dominate the industrial sector, the government is developing new manufacturing centers. Wuhan, the site of China's second largest steel plant, is expected to achieve an annual output of two million tons.

The production of silk fabric, one of China's most ancient crafts, is now a major industry. Since 1949 silk-making methods have been modernized. Yet much of the delicate work required to raise silkworms—whose fragile cocoons provide the raw material for silk thread—is still done by hand. Mills receive spools of silk thread and, using automatic power looms, weave the fibers into strong, lightweight cloth.

Courtesy of F. Botts/FAO

Young silkworms *(left)* feed on the leaves of mulberry trees. When fully grown, silkworms stop eating and spin a cocoon (an outer wrapping). Factory workers *(bottom left)* sort the cocoons before the process of reeling begins. Reeling involves unwinding the flimsy silken threads of the cocoon to form stronger strands. The strands are processed further to provide the raw material for silk weaving. Powerful looms *(bottom right)* transform the threads into shiny, lightweight cloth.

Photo by Mirjam van der Heyden/Charlie Rabelink

Courtesy of Mark Anderson

Transportation and Energy

With such a vast area to cover—much of it inaccessible—railways are by far China's most important long-distance form of transportation. Rail connects all of the nation's main cities and carries freight and passengers. Thirty thousand miles of track now crisscross the country, and in the 1980s short electric railways operated within some major cities.

Until World War II, China had seven highways. Four ran from north to south and three from west to east. Since 1950 the PRC has built many roads in parts of the country where no routes had previously existed. Some of the roads—such as those in Xizang and near the Indian border—were constructed for military purposes. Highways that carry trucks and buses link major cities. By the late 1980s unpaved roads connected almost every town in China. Few Chinese own cars, and most transportation is accomplished on foot or on bicycles.

The main rivers are still useful highways for both people and goods. Ocean freighters can travel up the Chang River as far

Independent Picture Service

Hairpin turns characterize the roads of remote mountain areas of China.

Independent Picture Service

The nation's many rivers—navigable for long stretches by small, flat-bottomed boats—are transportation routes for food and other goods.

Railway cars are filled with coal from northeastern China's abundant fields in the provinces of Liaoning and Jilin.

as Wuhan—640 miles from the sea—and from there river steamers can proceed to Chongqing. Smaller craft—junks and sampans (flat-bottomed boats with sails)—can continue farther still. Boats take manufactured goods upriver from Shanghai and Wuhan and bring down cotton, silk, vegetable oils, wool, hemp, tea, wheat, and tobacco.

Formed in 1988, Air China now handles China's air traffic. The airline established routes that crisscross China and that link the nation to many parts of the world. Air China flies to India, Pakistan, the Soviet Union, Western Europe, Japan, and the United States.

China has abundant sources of energy in its coal deposits and oil reserves and in the hydropower potential of its rivers. There are also substantial amounts of natural gas in the Sichuan Basin. Coal-fueled plants generate most of the nation's electricity, and some hydroelectric facilities—on the Huang and Han rivers, for example—have been built. Many small communities have their own water-pow-

A sampan—a small, oared craft—glides past fields planted along the Chang River.

ered generators. The number of people with electricity in their homes, however, is unevenly distributed between the populous eastern and the poorer western parts of the country.

Future Challenges

China faces great challenges in the coming decades. Its huge population—although restrained by law from adding substantially to its numbers—still pressures the agricultural sector, which operates on relatively little land. Relations with the Soviet Union improved in the 1980s, but tensions still exist between the two nations.

Decades of propaganda that discredited both Western ideas and China's past have given way to the embrace of Western technology, profit incentives, and foreign revenues. These new policies illustrate China's efforts to modernize its economy and to provide its people with a better living standard. Nevertheless, the nation walks a fine line between the Western economic doctrines it has long rejected and the Communist and socialist principles that have shaped it since 1949.

Crowds gather for a Communist rally at Tian'anmen Square in the 1970s. This same historic place hosted massive student demonstrations in the spring of 1989, when thousands of young Chinese asked for an end to political corruption and for greater political freedom.

Independent Picture Service

Courtesy of Mark Anderson

Billboards advertising the newest electronic equipment from Japan have appeared in the wake of China's new economic policies. Some observers feel that the rapid growth of Chinese demands for Western consumer goods and for economic prosperity have outpaced the country's ability to meet those expectations in the near future.

Index